About the Author

Leanne Renaud was born in September of 1969. She has five wonderful children and has three grandchildren. When she was young she suffered a very traumatic life. Due to the trauma in her life she now have PTSD. Since her thirties she has learnt and studied the laws of attraction. This has helped her in a lot of ways. She now looks at life optimistically and looks forward to each and every day. She is also somewhat of an artist. She designs and creates jewelry and makes dream catchers and lots of other creative ideas.

Passion for Poetry

Leanne Renaud

Passion for Poetry

Olympia Publishers
London

www.olympiapublishers.com
OLYMPIA PAPERBACK EDITION

Copyright © Leanne Renaud 2024

The right of Leanne Renaud to be identified as author of
this work has been asserted in accordance with sections 77 and 78 of
the Copyright, Designs and Patents Act 1988.

All Rights Reserved

No reproduction, copy or transmission of this publication
may be made without written permission.
No paragraph of this publication may be reproduced,
copied or transmitted save with the written permission of the publisher,
or in accordance with the provisions
of the Copyright Act 1956 (as amended).

Any person who commits any unauthorized act in relation to
this publication may be liable to criminal
prosecution and civil claims for damage.

A CIP catalogue record for this title is
available from the British Library.

ISBN: 978-1-80439-268-3

This is a work of fiction.
Names, characters, places and incidents originate from the writer's
imagination. Any resemblance to actual persons, living or dead, is
purely coincidental.

First Published in 2024

Olympia Publishers
Tallis House
2 Tallis Street
London
EC4Y 0AB

Printed in Great Britain

Dedication

I'd like to dedicate this book to my five children I treasure so much. And my three grandchildren who give me so much joy in my life.

Acknowledgements

I'd like to thank my dear friend Debbie Laventure who made some contributions to some of my poems. I'd also like to thank my friends and family who listened and helped me with some of the editing of my poems. They all gave me the courage to continue with my writing. Blessings to all.

Count My Blessings

As I wake up every morning
I think of all I want to do.
I go downstairs to have my coffee
Getting ready for a day that's new.

As I rush to get things together
For another day of work
I realize something I forgot
And it will make me go berserk.

Luckily this thing that I forgot
I can do almost anywhere.
I need to count my blessings
To start my day without a care.

I thank God for all I have
And all the things I do
For all my family and friends
And this brand new day too.

You see it's important to count my blessings
And appreciate all I have
So everyday feels special
And I start it being glad.

Leanne Renaud LER69
04/21/2022

Thinking about You

When I wake up in the morning
All I do is think about you
You're on my mind everyday
And in my heart too.

When I look at your picture
A smile comes to my face.
It doesn't take me very long,
To go back to that place.

The place where my memories,
Of Us are so real.
Like the last time you touched me
And the way you made me feel.

The strength of my love for you
Can never be broken
For the love we have together
Can leave our words unspoken.

When we hold each other closely
As I look into your eyes.
I know we belong together
It comes as no surprise.

When you're not around me
I long for your touch
You're always in my heart
Because I Love You so much…

Leanne Renaud LER69
Debbie Laventure DML
04/23/2022

Opening My Life to a New Beginning

When I was young, I was afraid of everything.
I started viewing my life very negatively.
Because of this, bad things kept happening.
Everything I tried to do just kept unfastening.
Failure was something that I became used to.
I really needed God, but didn't know what to do.

One day God spoke to me,
In my time of pain and suffering
He told me, that if I told my abuser,
"I Love Him."
It would stop my pain.
I said, "I love you," repeatedly
And then the beating stopped.

From that day forward I knew God
Loved me and gave me the opportunity to escape my abuser
within inches of my life.

When I was 30, the Spirit breathed Life into me.
It was on St. Patrick's day
I felt a closeness to God that never went away.
I knew of things that I had no previous knowledge about
before.
Through the Spirit of God I was being moved inside my

very core.

Now that I'm 52, I find I fondly look back.
At all the things the Spirit showed me to help put me on the right track.
Life has been good to me, with many future possibilities.
I learned that, without the help of God,
My future would be very bleak.

So when I tell you that
God Loves You
I am speaking the truth
God loves all his children
On our planet Earth.

Leanne Renaud LER69
02/01/2022

Singing Praise for the Spirit

When you're down and out and you don't know what to do.
Praise the Lord for He always comes through.
Through His Spirit He will guide you all the way.
Life's a lesson every day.
The Spirit always listens when we pray.

We are angels of the Lord from thy birth.
We love and honor our planet Earth.
Love the painting of a circle green and blue.
For the children of the world, me and you.
For the Spirit will always come through.

With our hard work, love and charity
We can help so many in need.
When you give from your heart it makes you feel
Like you're given the comfort of a meal.

Singing praise for the Spirit, yes indeed.
Let us pray for the children in need.
In need...

Leanne Renaud LER69
Debbie Laventure DML

My Precious Shining Star

The morning when I first found out
In nine months you'll arrive.
I was so excited about meeting you
The thrill made me feel alive.

I started preparing for your arrival
With anticipation for your birth.
With my excitement and love for you
I couldn't wait to see you on earth.

Every time you moved inside me
I knew you were as healthy as can be.
Can't wait until the day I see you.
So I can hold you once you're free.

On the day of your arrival,
When I saw your tiny face.
I was overwhelmed with love and joy.
In my arms you were placed.

When I looked into your eyes
The sweetest infant that you are.
I knew you'd always be
My precious shining star.

Leanne Renaud LER69

Spring Is Finally Sprung

The snow has melted and spring has sprung
The mating season has just begun
The birds and geese have all come back
To raise their young in their habitats.

Here in Canada we love the spring
It brings an abundance of everything
The birds all sing their morning songs
And before you know it the days are long.

The smells are lovely as the first flowers grow
We are all so happy that there is no more snow
So when we hear the birds singing to their young
We know that spring has finally sprung.

LeanneRenaud LER69
04/18/2022

Mom

In my heart you'll always be
A special woman for our family.
I wouldn't trade you for a million bucks
Even if I was down on my luck.

When I was younger, you were always there.
To show me love and that you cared.
You picked me up, when I was down.
Cheered me up when I had a frown.

You stuck by me through thick and thin.
You inspired me to begin.
To love and trust and never cease
You're a heavenly angel of inner peace…
I LOVE YOU MOM…

Leanne Renaud LER69

Dad

I always looked up to you
Because you are so strong
You always took the time
To teach me right from wrong.

When I was really young
You tucked me in at night.
You'd kiss me on the cheek
And hugged me oh so tight.

You taught me so many things
We had a lot of good times.
That's why I think
You're always on my mind.

You were so understanding
You had a magic touch.
All I want to say to you
Is I love you so, so much.

Leanne Renaud LER69
06/11/2022

Autumn Splendor

Driving down the back town roads
If you could only envision what I see.
An abundance of beauty and colors
In all the colorful leaves in the trees.

Around the bend a field of wild flowers
Swaying with the breeze.
A distant haze of blue and purple,
A painting it should be.

As we drive by a mirrored reflection
Driving down to Golden Lake.
We see an eagle in the distance
A picture we'd love to take.

In Canada our autumn
Is as beautiful as can be.
So come to Canada and join us
We'd love everyone to see.

Leanne Renaud LER69

Debbie Laventure DML
04/21/2022

A Long Time Coming

A very long time ago the Spirit spoke to me
In my time of darkness.
I was told to be strong and to never give up
That life was as precious as a beautiful melody.

I was given a new chance to view my life differently.
I was given a view of what my future could hold for me.
I felt the Spirit's Love unconditionally.

I learned about a secret called 'The Law of Attraction.'
But things just kept happening, with many distractions.
Life went on, but I always felt lonely
I yearned for a good friend.
Someone who'd be my one and only.

Many friends have come and gone over the years.
But I still believed I'd find that special friend in spite of all that.
I never gave up on finding a friend that would be there for me.

Last summer a wonderful woman introduced herself to me.
As I got to know her, I came to figure out that we are both artists among many other things we have in common.

I believe I found my new best friend.
I feel in my heart that I have found my soul sister.
A friend to the very end.

Thank you Great Spirit for sending your angel's in my time of need.
With my soul sister by my side, I know we will succeed
In helping those in need.

Leanne Renaud LER69

A Brand New Friend

Sometimes in life, we need a friend
Someone who can stick it out to the very end.
Someone who can laugh and cry with you
Someone who enjoys the same things as you do.

I made a new friend this very year.
With joy in my heart that I'm willing to share.
My friend is different but the same.
We have both suffered very similar pain.

We are friends cut from the same cloth.
We are definitely like two peas in a pod.
We are soul sisters; indeed we are.
I think I've finally found that magical star.

Leanne Renaud LER69
01/27/2022

Let Us Honor a Farmer

He's up at dawn to do his chores.
He works so hard, but never keeps score.
He feeds the animals and milks the cows.
He starts his tractor to go and plough.

A farmer's work is never done.
It's been his passion since he begun.
He's proud of his profession.
With very noble intentions.
He's kind and humble, I must say.
He wears a smile every day.

Look at the food that we eat
And think of where it came.
Let us honor a farmer, past and present.
And give him his claim to fame.

Leanne Renaud LER69
02/02/2022

The Love I Have for You

It's the first eyes that you see in the morning.
The Love you have when they look at you
The excitement when given their morning meal.
Their wiggling tails prove their love is true.

Their anticipation for their morning walk
The excitement when they see a friend
The kisses that never stop
Because they will love you to the very end.

A dog and cat are not only pets
They are family and our best friends
Loving them should come easily
Let us care for them to the very end.

Leanne Renaud LER69
04/19/2022

The Smile on Your Face

The smile on your face when I see you
Means more than you could know.
When you talk about your past life
You tell me your story with a glow.

You truly are so special
I love you so, so much.
I know your love for me is real.
I can feel it in your touch.

So please my dearest friend
Trust me when I say
God is always listening
When He hears you pray…

Your energy is calming
And you're as real as can be.
When I am around you
I feel so awesome and free.

Leanne Renaud LER69
04/20/2022

Missing You

Years ago when we were young
We laughed and played and had so much fun.
We knew we were different but never complained.
Our lives together were quite the same.

Yes dear sister, I speak of you.
Even though we're at odds
I still love you.
I wish you could love me like I love you.
My heart is sad and I miss you too.
So if you'll please forgive me for what I said.
I've forgiven you as I felt the dread.
My guilt I felt made me feel
Like I really would love us to heal
I love you my sister…

Leanne Renaud.LER69

The Spirit Within

The spirit lives inside of us
For those of us who seek.
Even for the ones who don't
Especially the meek.

In our lives we experience
Happiness and pain.
Without these experiences
We would have no gain.

We are here to live our lives
And learn lessons on earth.
So when we get to heaven
It's like a brand new birth.

Leanne Renaud LER69

My Dearest Friend

When I was in the worst place possible
You were always there.
We shared so many memories
I knew you always cared

You were so, so special with your charming ways.
You were the one who always made my day
Trust me when I say to you, my love for you will never go away.
Even though you're now in heaven
I'll love you every day.

My heart is with your family.
It'll never be the same
They will always be in my prayers.
A heavenly angel, you will remain

Leanne Renaud LER69

Yet You Say You Love Me

How can you say you love me
When you contradict yourself in every way.
In my times of sadness
You do not come to comfort me
Instead you show your anger
Or simply just walk away

When I tell you that I'm hurting
You twist the words of what I'm trying to say
So that you don't have to feel guilty
When you show your anger and walk away

Yes my heart is breaking
But I am finally giving up
You have never offered to talk about it
So I've finally realized I've had enough.

And yet you tell me that you love me
But that love cannot be true.
Because if you did, you would fight for me.
And you won't, that is something I always knew.

How can you say you love me
When you don't even love yourself

Because if you did you would be happy.
And not the person you are now.

Leanne Renaud LER69

The Angel in All of Us

She takes the time to say hello
She takes the time to say goodbye
She takes the time to say the words
That makes your heart feel like smiling.

Her love will never go away, no matter what you do.
Her strength comes from her father in heaven
Who will always love you too.

She takes the time to plant a seed
Because that's what she does best.
She loves and trusts her father in heaven
And leaves him to do the rest.

If you look real hard
You'll find the angel that you seek
Because she lives inside of you
All you need to do is peek.

Leanne Renaud LER69

I Honor You with the Best of My Bud

God gave us grass
God gave us birds
God gave us the privilege of making out words.

We have oceans and we have land.
We have amazing plants that make life grand.
But most of all my favorite plant is actually a weed.
We call it Marijuana
It makes you feel good indeed.

If you were to come to my humble abode.
It would be an honor to have you as my guest
Especially to offer you a smoke of my very best.

This bud that I offer you is certainly my best.
It may even help you feel better,
Or give you some well-deserved rest.

So rest assured if you feel you are drowning in a flood
Always remember "I honor you with the best of my bud."

Leanne Renaud LER69

Speaking the Truth

Sometimes you feel stuck in life
We start feeling depressed with no end in sight.
You might be so down you feel really stuck.
Well I'm here to tell you you're just in luck.

I'd like to talk to you about a Great Secret.
That will help you get out of that very deep rut.
When I tell you this Secret I speak the truth
Once you hear it, you'll be feeling your youth.

This Secret is the Law of Attraction
When you figure it out you will put it in action
You can overcome your past and present situation.
So your future is full of unlimited creations.

You start by thinking of what you'd like your future to be.
There really is no limit to the possibilities.
You should always feel grateful for what you have now.
For that's when the universe figures out how.

You need to have the greatest desire.
And put it in action for all to admire.
No matter what you're wishing for
Even if it's money galore.
You can change your life using your thoughts.

No matter what you would like
Or what you were taught.

Start researching The Secret with books and documentaries,
And before you know it, your life will start changing with the greatest of ease.
So trust me when I tell you I'm speaking the truth
It's the Law of Attraction that continues to define you.

Leanne Renaud LER 69

A Rose Is Like No Other

I can remember a long time ago
My favorite job was going bar to bar
Selling my all-time favorite flower
Beautiful roses is what they are.

My route was Bank Street in Ottawa
I loved this route so much,
I made a lot of money
Because I had a special touch.

Many people bought them
Because a rose is like no other
Especially the men that were drunk
In hopes of finding a lover.

By the end of the evening
I traveled over to Quebec
To sell the rest of my roses
I figured what the heck.

I loved this job so much
It built confidence in me
To sell my favorite flowers
I was as honored as can be…

Leanne Renaud LER69
05/03/2022

Especially Made for You

This friendship bracelet that I made
With different colors and a braid.
I added charms to make it special
Which were made of shiny metal.

A charm for peace and one for love
A silver cross and a morning dove.
I added a four leaf clover for luck
And a paw print for a cat or pup.

This gift is especially made for you
Because I care and love you too.
I give it to you with all my heart
In hopes you'll remember me when we're apart…

Leanne Renaud LER69
Debbie Laventure DML
04/30/2022

Summer's Glory

Sitting on my step one day
There was a rainbow in the sky.
As I looked a little more
A flock of geese were flying by.

I see many people walking dog's
Children playing and having fun
The aroma of a barbeque
Everyone enjoying a little sun.

Yes, summer is finally here
And the days are getting warmer
Let's enjoy it while we have it
Because autumn is around the corner.

Leanne Renaud LER69
Debbie Laventure DML
04/30/2022

Our Dream

I dream of opening a store
This year of '22.
I hope I'm not biting off
More than I can chew.

On the other hand
Nothing ventured nothing gained.
I have a good feeling this is
Our claim to fame.

With my amazing partner and I
We know this business will soar and fly
Like the eagles in the sky.

With a smile from both of us
We welcome you to discuss
How to teach you with ease
With both our expertise.

With handmade gifts and art galore
You'll be coming back for more.
Thank you Great Spirit
With All Our Hearts.
For giving Us this brand new start.

Leanne Renaud LER69
Debbie Laventure DML
01/20/2022

Give with All Your Heart

Feeling good is a way of being
Sometimes it's hard to do.
It takes time to change the way of seeing
A challenge at first, even for you.

Every morning I thank the Spirit
For giving me a brand new day.
I give thanks for all the little things
That we usually take for granted, when I pray.

When you look at life in gratitude
Your life just starts to change.
Gifts come in a multitude,
At first it feels quite strange.

Joyfulness starts happening
You start looking forward to each and every day.
Forgiveness comes more easily
Once you form the habit to pray.

The best feeling is when you can help someone, anyone at all.
By giving your time or listening to what they have to say.
Sometimes you can give them a brand new start

When you give with all your heart.

Leanne Renaud LER69

Angels Really Do Exist

I believe angels are here
To help us when we live in fear.
No matter what the problem is
It may be something someone says.

They can come from anywhere.
when your life is in despair.
It can be a stranger or a friend
That may help you in the end.

Angels guide us everyday
With God's true love in every way.
They grace us with love and speed
In our darkest hours of need.

Ask for an angel that is heaven sent
And before you know it, you'll be on the mend
So if you're desperate and in need
Your angel will help you to succeed.

Please always remember this
Angels really do exist

Leanne Renaud LER69
04/28/2022

Stoned

I've lost my train of thought
What was I supposed to do.
What was I even thinking of
Everyone is looking at me too.

I hope I'm not being paranoid
I'm feeling that kind of dread.
I really started believing
I'm hearing voices in my head.

When is this feeling going to stop
Why is this trip so long?
Why didn't I listen to my parents
When they tried to teach me right from wrong…

Leanne Renaud LER69
Debbie Laventure DML
04/27/2022

On the Train to Nowhere

I don't even want to wake up in the morning
I feel there's nothing I'd like to do.
Thoughts are racing through my head
And I'm always feeling blue.

There really seems to be no end
To the hardships and the pain.
I really don't see any change
And it's driving me insane.

I feel I'm on a train to nowhere.
It's the end of the line for me.
I really don't want to be here.
Maybe dying will set me free.

As I contemplate my suicide.
I decide a bridge will be my fate
On a wall as I'm walking
There is a message saying WAIT.

I've been in your shoes
and yes, there is help to be given.
Trust me when I say to you.
That your life is worth living.

Everyday changes and can bring you something new.
If desperate phone this number
They will definitely help you.

SUICIDE HELP LINE CANADA
1-833-456-4566

Leanne Renaud LER69
Debbie Laventure DML 04/27/2022

Please Think Positive

Sometimes days don't go the way we want them to.
Sometimes it's something we regret saying to someone we once cared about.
Once we've said it, it's too late to take it back.
It could be your brother or sister or your best friend, it might be even your parents or child.
We've all been there at one time or another.
Taking the time to think before you speak, is very hard to do.
You can take the long road and in time it might be forgotten.
Or apologize, and hope for forgiveness.
But I choose to talk to the Spirit and ask for help to bite my tongue when people are getting rude.

You see with the Laws of Attraction, you really need to keep your cool.
What you say to someone in anger can make it harder for your dreams to come true.
Whatever way you act will attract more people acting the same way you feel.
What we think about with the most desire is what we attract into our lives.
Anger is a strong emotion, once it happens sometimes it's hard to get back on track.
So if you're feeling angry at something someone said.

Think about the damage it does to you before you start feeling the dread.
Thoughts become things,
So please think positive.

Leanne Renaud LER69

Loving Nature Sets Me Free

I couldn't wait for spring this year
When it finally came, I did a cheer.
I love gardening so, so much.
They say I have that special touch.

Planting seeds is what I know
Sometimes I plant them in a row.
With some rain and sunshine too
Brings me flowers that are so new.

When everything begins to bloom
The air starts smelling like sweet perfume.
With a pallet of colors that all can see
Loving nature sets me free.

A bouquet of flowers is what I pick
For my best friends, would do the trick.
My friends and I start to celebrate.
Nature's beauty we appreciate.

Leanne Renaud LER69
Contributions from Debbie Laventure DML

Pray for Help for Ukraine

This man of great power
Sent out his armed forces:
He decided he wanted Ukraine.

Most Ukrainians cried
And many had died
A lot of them suffered great pain.

Let the suffering cease
All we want is peace.
Let us pray for help for Ukraine…

Leanne Renaud LER69
Debbie Laventure DML
05/07/2022

In This Small Town

As I was walking down the street one day
I was watching the squirrels run and play.
In the distance I saw only three
Once I got closer, they scurried up a tree.

As I walked a little more
Because I was going to the store
I came across a lazy cat
So I decided to give him a little pat.

A little further I heard a melody
Of birds singing in the trees.
Around the corner the lilacs bloom
Giving off a smell like sweet perfume.

At my destination I finally arrive
The wonders of nature are so alive.
How grateful I feel in this small town
Loving the beauty that's all around.

Leanne Renaud LER69
Debbie Laventure DML
04/28/2022

You Are Always There

Sometimes you bring me a coffee
Which starts my day off right.
You are always there for me
You're such a beautiful sight.

We can talk about anything
At any given time.
We never have a problem
Speaking what's on our mind.

Whenever I felt I needed you
You were always there.
I know I can count on you
Because you really care.

The comfort I feel around you
Will never go away.
I truly love you dearly
In my heart you'll stay…

Leanne Renaud LER69
Debbie Laventure DML
05/02/2022

Down at the Park

Down at the park in Arnprior
On a Sunday afternoon
You could hear the music playing
An old angelic tune.

Children gather by the pavilion
Patiently waiting their turn
For the lady with paint and brushes
Face painting is what they yearn.

Everyone lining up outside
On a bright warm sunny day.
Listening to the music
While children run and play.

A good time is what we had,
A picnic at the park.
The hours went by so fast
It' started getting dark.

We gathered our belongings
And started walking home.
So together we were inspired
To write this little poem.

Leanne Renaud LER69
Debbie Laventure DML
05/01/2022

Angel Wings in Flight

I always light a candle
When I think of you
The thoughts always comfort me
For our love was true.

I look at our photo albums
And cry myself to sleep.
I'm in total anguish
All I do is weep.

Friends have come to comfort me
But sadness I still feel
Not long ago you we were with me
They tell me time will heal.

Sometimes I look forward to
The time we reunite
We'll both be in heaven
With our angel wings in flight.

Leanne Renaud LER69
Debbie Laventure DML
05/01/2022

Sunday Afternoon Drive

Looking at trees and rolling hills
On a Sunday afternoon drive.
Breathing in the air so fresh
It makes me feel alive.

The scenery of old barns and churches
Driving through small towns.
I took a moment to see the beauty
And heard a melody of sounds.

As we drive along the highway
We see farmers ploughing fields.
A sign that says, 'eggs for sale'
So we decide to stop for a deal.

As we approach another town
A chip truck is what we see.
With our stomachs feeling hungry
We decide to stop and eat.

When we arrive at our destination
Golden Lake is where we are.
With the beauty that surrounds us.
It really 'doesn't seem so far.

Leanne Renaud LER69
Debbie Laventure DML
05/01/2022

Praise the Lord We're Heading Home

I was on my fishing boat one night
Stormy seas made me lose my sight.
As the boat rocked and waves crashed.
I realized we were being smashed.

It was twilight hour and raining hard.
Everyone was on their guard.
We were pretty far out at sea
Getting back home was the key.

The crew worked hard with all their might
And in the distance we saw a light.
It was a lighthouse on the western shore
Delighted we were to the very core.

We set our sails towards the light
Thanking God with our delight.
The boat heads course, with a steady roam.
Praise the Lord, we're heading home…

Leanne Renaud LER69
Debbie Laventure DML
05/01/2022

My Soul Mate from Above

Sometimes I feel lonely
I long for someone to love.
I am still looking forward to
My soul mate from above.

I've had a few relationships
Those experiences were bad.
I look at them as lessons
So I don't have to be so sad.

Some day I know I'll find you
Whoever you may be.
I hope it's sometime soon
Because I see you in my dreams.

I hope I meet you this year
I bet you hope so too.
I can feel it coming closer
My dreams are coming true.

Leanne Renaud LER69
05/19/2022

Joy in Life Comes Naturally

As I wake up every morning
I thank God for another day.
I treasure every breath I breathe
For another day I get to play.

Joy in life comes naturally
Forgiveness is the key.
It's all about your attitude
I'm sure you would agree.

I'm blessed with many abilities
Like healing the ones in need.
Slowly people are understanding
It starts with a smile to proceed.

I have many people in my life
I call them family and friends.
This is why every day is a blessing
Their kind words always mend.

My feelings heal quite easily
When I'm hurting, it never lasts.
I know I need to remain thankful
And not think about the past.

I try to always have good vibes
And I smile a lot too.
I say hi to strangers
And help people feeling blue.

But most of all I try to stay happy
Even when things seem hard.
Just being very thankful
Keeps you in the best regards.

Leanne Renaud LER69
04/19/2022
Revised 05/17/2022

Embrace Your New Life

Life is hard, so I've been told
Sometimes happiness is hard to hold.
Yes, I agree, life isn't always easy
Because our past lives weren't so pleasing

Sometimes we worry about the future
We can't see life with any humor.
It gets depressing when you feel stuck
You may even feel like you're in a rut.

I have good news, just for you
It may even stop you from being blue.
The way your feeling can be changed
It's just your thoughts that you rearrange.

You start by appreciating what you have,
Which makes the universe very glad.
Then you concentrate on the things you'd like,
Feel you have them within your sight.

After a while things start to change
Soon your life just turns a page.
Things just get better than before,
Many opportunities and opened doors.

You got used to always feeling blue.
Now that is something you have to undo.
So put a smile on your face
Welcome a new life to embrace.

Leanne Renaud LER69
05/11/2022

I'll Love You Everyday

Maybe it's the way you look at me
Or the funny things you do.
It could be those beautiful eyes
Is the reason I love you.

No, the more I think about it
It's definitely the things you say,
Like the words "I love you so"
When we cuddle every day.

If I could only count the reasons
Why I love you so.
There isn't enough time in a day
And my words would overflow.

Trust me that my love is true
And will never go away
You're the best reason
I'll love you every day.

Leanne Renaud LER69
05/11/2022

Life Through Rose Colored Glasses

Wouldn't it be nice to see
A life with many possibilities?
Well, you can if you try
It only starts with a little smile.

You have to look at life differently
And think of your life wonderfully.
Be thankful that you're so blessed
And try to always feel the best.

Think of the things that you'd like
And feel it with your heart's delight.
Life changes when you try
Your outlook on life is the reason why.

Yes, you are in control of your life,
You really don't have to live with strife.
Thanking the Spirit is a really good start.
Feeling the love from deep within your heart.

I view my life through rose-colored glasses.
Because life gives me many chances.
Opportunities and love galore
There really is so much to explore.

Your new life is around the bend
Tell your children and your friends.
So put a smile upon your face
Get ready to accept love's embrace.

Leanne Renaud LER69 05/08/2022